To Savba

May your trust, hope & faith
in God be Increased
Enjoy the read
God bless you.

Knox

SEVENTY

A Work in Progress

1 2 3 4 5 6 7
8 9 10 11 12 13 14
15 16 17 18 19 20 21
22 23 24 25 26 27 28
29 30 31 32 33 34 35
36 37 38 39 40 41 42
43 44 45 46 47 48 49
50 51 52 53 54 55 56
57 58 59 60 61 62 63
64 65 66 67 68 69 70

DARA KNOX HOOKE

© KNOX Publications

Published by KNOX Publications
Copyright © Dara Knox-Hooke 2015
The moral right of the author has been asserted.
www.daraknox.com

Photograph courtesy of the author.
Illustration's by Lenahrose
www.lenahrose.com

All rights reserved.
Without limiting the rights under copyright reserved above, no part of this publication may be reproduced, stored in or introduced into a retrieval system, or transmitted, in any form or by any means (electronic, mechanical, photocopying, recording or otherwise), without the prior written permission of the copyright owner of this book.

ISBN: 978-0-9934495-0-5

Scripture quotations are taken from:
The Holy Bible. New King James Version (NKJV).
Copyright @1982 by Thomas Nelson, Inc. All rights reserved.

The Authorized (King James) Version. Rights in the Authorized Version in the United Kingdom are vested in the Crown. Reproduced by permission of the Crown's patentee, Cambridge University Press

Scriptures and additional materials quoted are from the Good News Bible© 1994 published by the Bible Societies/HarperCollins Publishers Ltd UK, Good News Bible© American Bible Society 1966, 1971, 1976, 1992. Used with permission.

To God's gracious gift
Zane

CONTENTS

1
Who Was I? 1

2
The Test 15

3
Get Behind Me, Satan 25

4
Numbers Don't Lie, Neither Does His Word 29

5
There is Power in the Tongue 37

6
The Day of Reckoning 43

7
God's Gracious Gift 61

Afterword 67

ACKNOWLEDGEMENTS

I first acknowledge and give thanks to my heavenly Father for the afflictions which brought about joy and gave me strength, and moulded me into the person I am today. I thank you in advance for I know your plan for me is to prosper.

I give thanks for my mother and my father here in this world, for all your words of encouragement, the discipline you incorporated. Even when I didn't listen, you never left me to my own devices. I especially thank my mother for staying on her knees praying for me; I pray God grants you your heart's desires.

I thank my spiritual mother and my reverend Comfort Leye for guiding me on my journey, for fighting battles with me and making time for me no matter the hour. God will surely uphold you till the very end. To the congregation at Salvation Sanctuary in Dagenham, Essex, who have heard my testimony, thank you for not judging me and embracing me instead.

Dinah and Daniela thank you for being there for me, for telling me the truth even if I didn't want to hear it, for repeatedly listening to me through my tears, and supporting me even in decisions you didn't agree with.

I thank JT for giving me a son. I give God thanks for every situation we went through, as it sharpened me as a person and set the pace for where I am going. God has used you immensely in my life for good, even when it seemed terrible. I count it all as joy.

I would also like to thank Bishop Wayne Malcolm for giving me the mic to share my testimony for the first time at Christian Life City, now known as iCan Ministries in East London. It encouraged me to write this book to share worldwide.

To every living soul reading this book right now, I thank you for investing in me. I pray this will open your eyes – even if by just a fraction – to the glorious things God can and will do for you, as He did for me.

To God be the glory.

INTRODUCTION

The first thing I want you to know is that you do not need to wait for change to come before you come to God. You will discover that trying to change yourself just doesn't seem to work. There is no crime too heinous, no filth filthy enough, and no scandal that's too scandalous to stop God from loving you. Exactly how you are at this very moment, He is there waiting for you to tag Him in. All of your loneliness, feelings of rejection, and addictions, He is ready to replace with comfort, acceptance and freedom.

I have written this book to share my testimony to the power of God as far as it can reach around the world, to allow you to read and feel the presence of God within the chapters. To show you that God doesn't call the qualified; instead, He qualifies the called. I was once a wretch, but with His redeeming grace and mercy, I can stand before my God and praise Him. Follow me through these pages to read my message, which was once a mess, and my test, which is now my testimony.

Therefore if any man be in Christ, he is a new creature: old things are passed away; behold all things are become new.

2 Corinthians 5:17 (KJV)

Chapter One

WHO WAS I?

Disobedient, disrespectful, and dishonest are just a few words I could use to describe myself before I was redeemed. I further add that I was a 'self-dependant' and 'self-righteous' 'know-it-all' – all the characteristics of an ungodly person – and I was more than happy revelling in these characteristics. I had a fiery attitude and would feel no inhibition in cussing people out to levels far beyond necessary.

All I needed was myself. I moved out of my mother's house at 18 and began life as a woman, paying rent and holding down a job. I also had a boyfriend. We actually first met at a christening when we were 10, and later, I used to see him at other neighbourhood functions. Fast forward to 18, and we started dating. He was everything I felt I needed in a man: he was handsome, popular, well-dressed, and he had a car. Besides myself, it was him that I worshipped; he was unknowingly my god. He gave me butterflies every single time I saw him. He struggled to look me dead in the eyes, which I put down to his 'shy'

SEVENTY

nature. I found it quite cute. I would've happily given up my property to go live in the creases of his clothes because they always smelt so good. He never had to be too sorry when he did me wrong. I would've jumped ten feet higher than the height he requested. There wasn't anything I wouldn't have done for him; I was that in love with him and craved that love back. Maybe I was searching for love from a man, love that I didn't get from my own father. I don't recall ever hearing 'I love you' from my dad. Perhaps that affected me later on in life.

My parents had a tempestuous relationship. I remember hearing the arguments and my mother take the punches; seeing her tears; seeing the other woman. Did I grow and subconsciously accept this as normal behaviour? Maybe.

My boyfriend went in and out of prison, and I, with low aspirations, wanted to be the ride-or-die chick. Despite the other girls he had floating about every so often, it was me who remained in waiting, running to his aid when trouble surfaced. I was so desperate for him to just love me, to give me the respect I knew in the back of my mind I deserved (because I did not demand nor openly beg him to 'respect' me), and to stop sharing himself with others. My love for him was at a point where I was more than willing to overlook his recent cheating and work our way through it. Instead, he rejected the idea of staying together and jogged down the staircase from my flat as quickly as he could.

Just to veer off the topic for a moment – I learned somewhere that perhaps the black box called the television that many are addicted to, or looking at other people's relationships, has encouraged this ridiculous idea of fighting tooth and nail for 'my man', and I mean literally, because over the years, some teeth were broken and nails were popped (none of them belonged to me by the way). This idea reinforces that as women, this is what we do and accept. Yes, men cheat, but don't all men? When it happens, cry and get over it. You stick with them: kick up a fuss, act like a bitch; he buys you flowers, shoes, and handbags. He says sorry and all is forgiven. At least this is what is shown quite often on television. Eventually, all the other women start to fade away, and like the rising Sun, he sees your glory and beauty and realises you are indeed 'the one'. Then you proceed to take the throne as Queen and the side chicks bow down before thee, and then disappear into the darkness they came from.

SEVENTY

Cue the record scratch and back to the topic at hand. This isn't, and wasn't, my reality; not only was there an absence of flowers, handbags, or shoes given in apology, he refused to stay with me even after I accepted his apology prior to its delayed arrival, and I gave him forgiveness, which at the time he didn't care for. As I proceeded to pick my jaw and sprinkles of the tiny specks of self-respect I had for myself off the floor, I decided to accept the fact that the relationship was over and I moved on. There's something about summertime – maybe its good weather and plenty of social gatherings – that makes you not care for a relationship too much or can distract you from heartaches. Let's all be honest and admit that this is, in fact, true.

I wasn't looking for another boyfriend or for anyone after my breakup. I was enjoying the weather and my job working in a mobile phone store. I made some good friends there, and with the commission and generous bonuses, the pay was actually very attractive.

Now on the subject of attraction. What transpired next from a mere comment I made to a friend who came to visit me at work to get a new phone, resulted in just that: attraction. I came across a picture whilst snooping in his mobile phone and briefly stopped, head tilted to one side, and asked the rhetorical question to no one in particular, *'Oh, who's that, he's cute?'* To my surprise, my curiosity was relayed back to the cute person in question, and he popped up at my work a few weeks later with my friend in tow. If looks could kill, I'd be guilty of murder in the third degree for the way I shot my friend with visual bullets. I mean, he could have warned me; perhaps I would have worn a shirt instead of a sweater. Maybe I would've opted for a side part instead of a middle part. I mean it would've been nice to have the option to look 'unintentionally' great. That's not to say I didn't look good, but you know, a sudden visit takes some mental preparation!

The guy was indeed good-looking; he was polite and soft-spoken and we conversed for quite some time, after which he asked for my number. We spoke every day since, and even though the dating didn't last very long, we remained friends.

Months had gone by and I hadn't seen my ex, and I was well and truly getting on with life. At times, I think it's easier to move on and for feelings to fade away, or in this case, which I am about to address, to lay dormant when you don't see the person. I thought things were well and truly finished between me and my ex, until one day to my surprise, whilst I was hanging out with a group of friends, he turned up.

Now, for the purpose of identifying who I am speaking about next, I am going to label them 1 and 2. I made a conscious decision not to include any names of men I dated in the body of this book and certainly didn't want to use fictional names either because this book is all truth. Number 1 is my ex. It makes sense to give him Number 1 for obvious reasons: he was here first, and at that time in my life, he was for sure my Number 1 even through the drama. So Number 2 would then be the new guy who, for that moment, had my attention, but due to Number 1's supreme spot, he could only ever be Number 2.

Okay, now back to what I was saying. So there we were, all hanging out at a mutual friend's house. I was sitting next to Number 2 among a group of others. There was a knock at the door and in came Number 1. I had not seen nor spoken to him in over two months, and to add to the surprise, Number 1 and Number 2 cordially greeted each other (black hole swallow me now). That moment was my cue to exit stage left and leave.

WHO WAS I?

As I sped home down the A12 motorway, various things came to mind. *How do they know each other? How well do they know each other? Number 1 looked gooooood. Am I now the topic of discussion? I should've stayed, this looks bad, but why would it be bad? You're single. Okay, calm down.* I parked outside my flat and ran upstairs to continue my what-the-heck session in my mind. As I put the key in the door, a message came through on my phone.

It was from Number 1. I was nervous to open it. *He's cussing me for sure*, I thought to myself. I unlocked my phone to face the harsh reality of a rude message. Instead, the text said, 'I miss you'. I paused and immediately began laughing; the laughing turned to dancing. I shuffled my feet around my hallway and began a full-blown shimmy, and finally jumped on my bed, kicking my feet about like a little school girl. I gave a dry response to hide my jubilation. We texted back and forth for a while, and I told him I had met someone else. He wasn't too pleased about it, but made it known that he was interested in reconciliation. I, too, was interested and agreed we could work on rebuilding our relationship.

I was happy he was back in my life and was looking forward to being back with my Number 1, so much so

SEVENTY

that I completely overlooked his cheating earlier on in the year. Besides, I had a new problem, and it wasn't another woman. He had a case against him that was more than likely going to result in more jail time.

I briefly wondered if he made his feelings to me known because he was going back to jail and wanted me to stand by him. I was also someone he trusted to look after his belongings whilst he was away. Whatever the case was, I was happy that he missed me, and I decided to get back into a relationship with him. I would have to wait to be with him again for approximately two-and-a-half years. But I accepted the challenge, and it wasn't too long before I messed that up.

You see, Number 2 and I were still friends; at least we thought we could be. In a moment of weakness Number 2 and I crossed boundaries, and I was now sitting in the dirty cheater's seat along with him – he was back with his girlfriend who was expecting their first child, and I had agreed to rebuild my relationship with Number 1. It was evident that friendship at this stage surely could not work, especially when feelings of like or lust were involved. My Number 1 learned that the tables had turned and I was now the cheater. He blamed himself for my behaviour and felt I acted this way for revenge, when that certainly was not the case. I apologised, I cried, and I begged for his forgiveness, but I quickly learned that he would not forgive me like I did him, and I simply took the harsh words and treatment that came my way. I felt like I had to earn his trust and prove myself loyal again. I even wanted to prove to myself that I was loyal and not a scandalous being.

    But in my effort to prove my point, I began to lose sight of myself. I lost my sense of self-respect and worth, and to be honest, that was already shaky prior to my cheating. Over the course of our ten-year relationship, I turned a blind eye to his actions many times; I overlooked the disrespect that came again in the form of a few other women who went in and out of our relationship. At times, I even justified it and looked at it like a free pass because of what I had done. I still told myself, *well it's been ten years together, and now, in June of 2014, at 29 years old, he must love me, because why else would he still be with me?* He would call me 'stupid', a 'follower', laugh at my dreams, and dishearten me. Being supportive and encouraging wasn't something he did, and I accepted it.

    I remember a time when he was taking a bath and I was standing in the doorway, telling him about my plans

SEVENTY

to be a fashion designer. I was so excited. I was explaining where I could see myself and how I wanted my brand to be, and he asked me, 'How will you get it out there?' *Good question,* I thought. I knew some people in the industry and a few who rubbed shoulders with celebrities, so I responded, 'Well, I know a few people in the industry. I also know a comedian who meets a lot of celebrities. Perhaps if I designed something for him that he liked, he could wear it, and I could get exposure that way.' The roars of laughter that came from my boyfriend made me feel like a comedienne that just told the funniest joke in the world, except I wasn't a comedienne, nor was I joking. Walking away from the bathroom doorway feeling embarrassed about the whole idea, I tried to wipe the dream of becoming a designer out of my head.

    The majority of what I have done in my life has been in the hopes of impressing my boyfriend and trying to make him see how much of a catch I was. In my head, I knew what I had to offer, yet my actions didn't mirror someone who knew themselves and their worth. Not knowing my value led not only to my boyfriend disrespecting me, but the girls he would cheat on me with to do the same. The level of humiliation I felt was unimaginable. I knew I should have walked away from him, yet I felt I had a point to prove to the world, and to myself, that this guy would love and respect me one day. My ears were blocked to the advice coming from everyone telling me to leave him.

The hurt seemed to have the opposite effect. Instead of making me walk away, it kept me hanging on. I was scared to walk away, and even though to everyone else he was never mine, I did not want to lose him. Even after he cheated again with another girl, I stayed. I thought to myself if I tried really hard to keep him happy and didn't put a foot wrong, he would realise my value and love me. Over time, I became scared of him. I didn't want to complain too much in case it resulted in him cheating. If he disrespected me, I would stick up for myself, but only to a small extent, because I didn't want to push him into the arms of another woman. So I would suck it up, smile, and act as though I was fine and none of his behaviour bothered me. At night I would cry; I would wonder if he was with someone else if he didn't answer his phone. I would feel unhappy being intimate with him because in my head, I would imagine him with these other girls and wonder what was wrong with me. I would question myself, wondering if I was as good as them or as attractive

SEVENTY

as them. Maybe my skin was too dark or I was too skinny. But if I refused intimacy, he would go elsewhere, so I maintained the relationship ensuring I met every one of his needs, even if my own weren't met.

My mother blamed my dysfunctional relationship on herself. She felt that I had grown to accept disrespectful behaviour because of what she put up with from my father. I thought my dad loved my mother, even though he abused her verbally, physically, and emotionally. He also had another woman. I perhaps grew up thinking this was love, that this was normal. So when faced with those three things myself, I didn't run from them. As confusing a feeling it was, I accepted it because whilst it didn't feel good, this was the love that I recognised. Seeing my mum cry for me broke my heart. I didn't want to be this insecure and weak person that allowed themselves to be walked over. I no longer wanted to be in such a messy place. Lies, weakness, cheating, promiscuity, and disrespect are not what I wanted to be associated with. Strength is what I needed. I had heard so much about God, so I started to seek Him and see what He was about.

my brethren count it all *joy* when you fall into various trials, knowing the testing of your faith produces patience. But let patience have its perfect work, that you may be **Perfect and complete,** lacking nothing.

James 1:2-4 (NKJV)

Chapter Two

THE TEST

My journey to find Christ began back in 2009, when I took the first step and got baptised after my mother, who was now a born again believer and well into her journey as a Christian and had been praying for years for all of her children to come to Christ. I was the first of my four siblings to take that step. My boyfriend was still in prison at the time, but life was good and I felt so full of joy. My bad attitude subsided. I felt completely renewed and refreshed after being baptised. However, I was not covering myself by reading the word of God, going to church regularly, or even praying. I thought I was saved, that my problems would be solved, and that was it.

Friends and folk, I tell you this: it is when you take that step closer to God that the devil will try to attack even more. Jesus himself was not exempt from the enemy's temptations, so who was I to avoid such tests? Satan is not bothered by the ungodly. Quite frankly, the ungodly are doing him a favour by rebelling against God. The ones who choose God are who Satan rises up against, even though the scriptures tell us in **Isaiah 54:17**:

No weapons formed against you shall prosper.
(NKJV)

    I have been working since the age of 16 in various roles in retail, from sales in the mobile phone store to banking, real estate, and insurance. But I always had a keen interest in fashion and began gaining experience in various fashion houses. In 2011, I began working as an international brand specialist in one of the world's most luxurious stores. My personal life, on the other hand, was anything but luxurious. I had more bills than money, and at the time, I was the only one working among all my siblings.
    I have always been one to help others even if I temporarily go without. My boyfriend was away in prison and had entrusted me to look after some money for him. Every now and then, when a bill dropped through my door, I would 'borrow' his money and replace it when I got paid. If I saw my mum struggling, I would help her too. But over the course of the 18 months he was gone, I had managed

THE TEST

to somehow spiral way out of control and realised I had spent a large sum of his money. My stomach was turning. *That's it. Ruined!* I thought to myself. I was so scared to tell him what had happened; I knew he would definitely flip out on me and leave me. I was determined to not let that happen. I needed to get back this money quick, and time was not on my side. I had about six months to make an average person's yearly salary. My credit wasn't the best at the time, so the banks were not interested. I felt like I had no other option and responded to offers from people I knew dabbled in fraud. I didn't want to do it on my doorstep in the UK, so I would travel abroad with my friend to purchase high-value goods and sell them to make cash.

In hindsight, choosing this way to help fix my problem was like taking the bait the enemy presented to me; and God permitted it to be so. I am not saying God wants us to do things wrong, but everything in life is permitted by God, for He is always in control. When we sin, it is not God's will. But He will allow things to happen for His glory to manifest. He will allow trouble and pain to bring about triumph and praise. He is the ultimate expert at bringing good out of bad.

SEVENTY

The Bible teaches us in **2 Corinthians 4:17**:

And this small and temporary trouble we suffer will bring us a tremendous and eternal glory, much greater than the trouble.
(GNB)

There are consequences of everything that we do, great or small, and the consequence of the path I chose landed me in prison in Austria. How could this be? How did I even get caught? I had become too good at the bad I was doing.

I had work the next day; I had a prison visit booked to see my boyfriend later in the week; I needed to return my mum's missed call. I hadn't even fixed the problem that got me doing fraudulent activities in the first place! But there I was, in a prison cell with ten other females, all smokers, and all staring at the one slim black girl in the room. In my head, tears were flowing and I was screaming for my mum, but I'd watched far too many movies to let these inmates think I was weak. So I employed my former bad attitude and stink face. I was preparing myself by fist and force that I would not be walked over.

THE TEST

I took a seat at the table that had a plate waiting for me; evidently these inmates were expecting a new guest. I looked into the bowl at what I could only describe as cat food – not the one in gravy, but the one in jelly mixed into pasta. The world around me disappeared. I began daydreaming about and appreciating the food I had wasted the night before in the comfort of my own home. My daydream didn't last long, as I was interrupted by a deep voice coming from behind me that said, 'What's your name?' I was tapping my foot on the floor, trying to mask the trembling of the rest of my body. I turned my head to answer. In a high-pitched squeaky voice that did not sound like me, I told her my name. *My nerves are showing, let me try that again*, I thought. This time I repeated myself with some bass and authority in my tone. She asked me why I was there. I briefly described the situation, and from the little that I shared with her, she came to the conclusion that I was screwed. She told me fraud and theft was a big deal in Austria, and especially as I was black, it would be worse. The next question she asked was, 'Do you know Hitler was born in Austria?' At that moment, my mind exited the conversation. I didn't need nor want to hear all of this. Surely this was a bad dream. As night fell, I silently cried myself to sleep, hoping it would all just be a horrible dream.

    I woke up the following morning at 6 AM and realised it was not a dream. I was thousands of miles away from home, facing a language barrier, without a support system. I had nothing but the clothes on my back. At least at the time I thought I had nothing. God was always there, but at the time of my arrest, He was the last thing on my mind.

    With all the free time I now had sitting in my cell, I didn't have time for God. I was busy looking for various (wrong) ways to try and get myself out of there fast. I offered bribes to the lawyer to release me, and he refused. When I realised I could not release myself through bribe and heard horror stories about the crazy sentences people were receiving for crimes far smaller than mine is when I humbled myself, turned to God, and began to pray and ask for forgiveness. For the scriptures state in **2 Chronicles 7:14**:

If my people, who are called by my name, will humble themselves and pray and seek my face and turn from their wicked ways, then I will hear from

THE TEST

heaven, and I will forgive their sin and will heal their land.
(NJKV)

    I would read the Bible daily, but not much would stick. I could remember lyrics to hip hop and RnB songs after hearing them once, but the words in the Bible would disappear from my memory as soon as I read them. As the days went by, as the severity of the situation became more apparent, and as the feeling of despair started to sink in, I read through the Bible page after page, seeking to know more and more. My dead spirit began to awaken, and I started to remember all the things my mother used to tell me about God and the prayers she would pray. One prayer I was familiar with and would constantly recite before I got my hands on a Bible in prison was the Lord's Prayer from the gospel of **Matthew 6:9-13**:

In this manner, therefore, pray:
Our Father in heaven,
Hallowed be Your name.
Your kingdom come.
Your will be done

SEVENTY

On earth as it is in heaven.
Give us this day our daily bread.
And forgive us our debts,
As we forgive our debtors.
And do not lead us into temptation,
But deliver us from the evil one.
For Yours is the kingdom and the power and the glory forever. Amen.
(NKJV)

I didn't realise at that time how paramount that prayer was. It covered a multitude of things. With this prayer, I asked God to give me what I needed daily and to forgive me as I have forgiven others; I asked to be free from evil and not be led into temptation. I told God that glory is His forever. You see, God knows exactly what we need before we even ask. He doesn't need us to repetitively ramble on for hours, thinking our prayers will be heard due to their length. Specific prayer and faith whilst praying are what work. Above all, they work only if it is God's will.

In the beginning, I hoped no one back home knew the shame I had brought on myself and my family, but then I realised I needed mass prayer. I spoke to my mum and I could hear she was troubled. She didn't sound like the strong woman of faith I knew her to be. She told me she had stopped going to church as she was embarrassed, but I urged her to tell the church not to be ashamed, to ask them all to pray for me together, for it states in God's word in **Matthew 18:20**:

For where two or three come together in my name, I am there with them.
(GNB)

get away from me, Satan! you are an obstacle in my way because these thoughts of yours don't come from God, but from human nature.

Matthew 16:23 (GNT)

Chapter Three

GET BEHIND ME, SATAN

I used to tell my mum that I didn't know how to pray. I used to think there had to be a certain tempo, a certain manner and fashion in which it should be done, and the few times I tried to pray, it lasted all but ten seconds because something would easily distract me and I would just give up. Yet here I was, digging deep into God's word and praying for myself.

One afternoon I was sitting in my cell, praying and reading my Bible notes. I could feel the presence of God upon me, the weight lifting off my shoulders, replaced by an immense feeling of comfort and love. This love was a love I had never ever experienced in my life: indescribable and difficult to put into words. It filled that void I sought to fill through my boyfriend – the missing piece to a puzzle. A mother's love or a man's love does not compare to this love that I could feel. Was a lying, thieving, unfaithful, idol worshipping, and disobedient wretch like me still loved? His presence hugged me and told me not to worry because I was forgiven and He loved me. That is where what I can only describe as the 'ugly cry' happened: my mouth turned upside down, lips trembling, face covered in snot. *Dara, you have to stop crying like this*, were my thoughts. Well, actually this was an exception as these were tears of joy.

But as soon as I felt and accepted God's love is when my open-air prayer was attacked with thoughts like *shut up, He doesn't love you, look at all the things you have done, you're staying here*. My mum who was back home, fighting spirit back, in effect praying for me down at the altar, prostrate position, crying out to God for me, was also under attack. The enemy kept telling her 'ten years'. The Bible states in **Luke 10:19**:

Listen, I have given you authority, so that you can walk on snakes and scorpions and overcome all of the power of the enemy, and nothing will hurt you.
(GNB)

It did not stop there. Various attempts were made to try and break my spirit. Rumours were flying about the prison that I was to remain there for a long time. The one letter that I was allowed to have from the UK was from someone who took the time to write and explain why they did not like me. The head officer in the prison confiscated the television in my cell because I didn't understand Deutsch when she spoke to me. She stopped me from using the telephone and also delayed my other letters. Through all of this, I remained calm. In fact, it was now a new habit to pray and bless those who did me wrong. I believed that God would take care of it all. His word taught me in **2 Thessalonians 1:6**:

God will do what is right, He will bring suffering on those who make you suffer.
(GNB).

From that moment on, the oppression I was facing at the hands of the head officer stopped, as she took sick leave for the rest of the time I was there.

God keeps every promise he makes. He is like a shield for all who seek his protection.

Proverbs 30:5 (GNT)

Chapter Four

NUMBERS DON'T LIE, NEITHER DOES HIS WORD

'Five years! They gave me five years,' were the cries I could hear coming from the corridor. I popped my head out of my cell, which was strangely left open, and watched her pace up and down the hallway, swearing and enraged at the sentence given to her. It was a girl from the cell next to mine. She had just been convicted of fraud. For a moment, if I'm honest, that was a little frightening to hear. I too was here on fraud charges and my court date was approaching soon. That nervous, sick feeling started lurking and I began to worry about what would happen to me on the day of my court hearing. I dared to question God's ability and began doubting the possibility of walking out of here anytime soon. I moved away from my cell door; it was such a disheartening sight to see and hear her cries. They only planted panic and doubt in my mind.

Looking back, I think it's fair to say that at times my faith was easily shaken. But when God is ready to act, nothing can stop Him. Sometimes, I would play this game

SEVENTY

I call 'flip the page', where I would flip open the Bible, and whatever my eyes landed on first would be something I believed God wanted to tell me. After seeing the girl so upset from receiving her five-year sentence, and with my upcoming court hearing, I needed the comfort of knowing I would be okay. I also realised that I needed some sort of structure in my search for a word from God, so I altered my normal game rules to focus on the numbers associated with my court date. The date of my hearing was 27 May – 27/5. I went to page 275 of my Good News Bible. This page took me to the book of 1 Samuel, Verse 12, and I looked at Verse 5, May being the fifth month. It said:

The Lord and the king he has chosen are witnesses today that you have found me to be completely innocent.
(GNB)

I frowned and tilted my head, thinking to myself, *are you teasing me?* It was a remarkable coincidence and one I was pleased with, but surely it was nothing more than that, so I tried another one. The book of Psalms was my favourite book in the Bible, so I went to Psalm 27, 27 being the day in the month of my court hearing and went to Verse 5, May being the fifth month of the year, and it said:

In times of trouble, he will shelter me; he will keep me safe in his temple and make me secure on a high rock.
(GNB)

This time I burst out laughing thinking, *all powerful and with a sense of humour is this God that I am getting to know.* I was convinced at this point that this perhaps was not a coincidence. I was pleased with my flip-the-page session and relaxed. But I tell you brothers and sisters, do not relax and veer from God's word because the enemy does not rest. The Bible tells us this in **1 Peter 5:8**:

Be alert, be on watch! Your enemy, the Devil, roams around like a roaring lion, looking for someone to devour.
(GNB)

SEVENTY

It wasn't long after the game before another worrying thought popped into my head. *What do I actually stand up in court to say?* Do I condemn myself, let the evidence speak for itself, or do I plead my innocence? *But what if they ask me to swear under oath?* I could not place my hand on the Bible to swear and then lie. I decided I would tell the absolute truth and whatever happened would happen. I would leave it to God. I felt happy knowing it would please God that I spoke the truth, but it would now mean that I for sure would not be going home anytime soon, so I felt sad at the same time.

I had got my television back after it had been confiscated and tried to cheer myself up by watching some in my cell, but I was not satisfied with the unsettling thought of potentially spending years in this cockroach-infested prison where they only allowed me to use the shower on Wednesday. So I began to pray and went in for another flip-the-page session, this time with the original rules: flip the pages, and the first thing my eyes land on would be for me. My eyes landed on the book of **Romans 3:3-4** when I read:

But what if some of them were not faithful? Does this mean that God will not be faithful? Certainly not! God must be true, even though all human beings are liars. As the scripture says, "You must be shown to be right when you speak; you must win your case when you are being tried."
(GNB)

I was astounded at how relevant this scripture was to my current situation but questioned whether I was being told to lie. I thought this couldn't possibly be true. So I continued praying over the matter some more when I read in **Romans 3:21-22**:

But now God's way of putting people right with himself has been revealed. It has nothing to do with law, even though the Law of Moses and the prophets gave their witness to it. God puts people right through their faith in Jesus Christ. God does this to all who believe in Christ, because there is no difference at all.
(GNB)

SEVENTY

From this second session of flip the page, I quickly learned that my God is no god of coincidence. What seemed to be random choices of scriptures were very relevant to my situation; not random at all. That was my direct confirmation that everything would be okay and God was with me. The way His plan for me was unfolding before my very eyes had my mind blown. He is a God of His word, and every single thing He says He will do, He will do. It is written in the book of **Isaiah 46:9-10**:

**Remember what happened long ago;
acknowledge that I alone am God
and that there is no one else like me.**

**From the beginning I predicted the outcome;
long ago I foretold what would happen.
I said that my plans would never fail,
that I would do everything I intended to do.**
(GNB)

Death and Life are in the power of the tongue, and those who love it will eat its fruit.

Proverbs 18:21 (NKJV)

Chapter Five

THERE IS POWER IN THE TONGUE

During my incarceration, I was not permitted to attend classes to learn Deutsch or to attend the prison church, even though I had made it known that I was a Christian. Instead, they would always skip my name each week and call for my friend, who I was arrested with. This used to upset and frustrate me because she was not a Christian. She was a Muslim. I would complain and ask why they allowed a Muslim to go to church when I was the Christian.

But that voice in my head would tell me to relax and remind me that God was in control. In hindsight, I can now see that God wouldn't have had it any other way. In her attending church, she converted to Christianity, and I, within the confinement of my cell walls, spent that much-needed alone time to be still and to continue to build my relationship with God.

On the last Sunday before my court hearing, I was sitting in my cell, when I heard my name being called down the hallway. I wasn't expecting a visit from my lawyer, nor was it time to go into the yard. With a confused face, I looked out my cell and saw the line of all the normal attendees for church. I didn't hesitate to run over to the line in excitement. *Finally!* I thought to myself as we walked through the different wings of the prison, including the men's wing.

When we arrived at the church, I was alert, sitting up straight, with a big smile ready to praise God and listen to the sermon. We sang two songs: *Kumbaya* - which, for anyone who isn't familiar with the song, is a simple appeal to God to come and help those in need - and *Let my people go*. If I ever needed further confirmation of what's to come concerning my court case, this was it, in song form. Everyone in the church was either talking amongst themselves or falling asleep, but I was rejoicing and singing at the top of my lungs. I meant business and believed every word I sang. I was in my own little bubble; head and hands raised to the sky, with my eyes closed. When the service ended and I opened my eyes, I found everyone staring at me, perplexed. Some asked why I was so happy in a place like this. Even the pastor, a self-confessed man of God, did not believe I would walk free on the day of my court hearing. He said to me, 'Yes, God is good, but this is Austria.' He told me he had never seen someone with such faith like me, which made me wonder why he was a pastor. I told him there are no 'buts' with God. God is good, and He is faithful, and through Him, all things are possible. I even told him that whilst I enjoyed the church service, this would, unfortunately, be the first and the last one I attended because the following Sunday, I would be in my own church back home in the UK giving my testimony. He shook his head, smiled, and looked at me unconvinced as I was led back to my cell.

The week of my court hearing arrived. I would normally fast every weekend during my time in prison. But this time, I wanted to fast the entire week prior to my hearing. I remember being deeply concerned with my appearance when I first arrived there, dressed in expensive designer clothes. I had my Brazilian weave and my jewellery on. But as time went on and God humbled me, I found myself cutting the weave out with a butter knife – I had Snoop Dogg cornrows – and had my family send me my raggedy house clothes from the UK, and even though I was not fed properly during my time in prison, God never allowed my appearance to be affected, which was something that I cared about greatly at that time.

My sister was even surprised when she visited me and commented that I still looked normal. That was indeed the case until I was two days into my fast: I remember standing in the mirror talking to God when I told Him I was no longer concerned with my appearance. From that day on, through my fast, I dropped a significant amount of weight. For someone who is 5 feet 7 inches and 8 stone 7 pounds on a good day, weight loss wasn't needed. I have always been slim, but I now appeared gaunt. I had taken on a frail and weak appearance.

But my faith was far from weak and my God far from frail. In fact, I was so certain I was going home that I gave away all of my belongings two days prior to my court hearing. People warned me not to do that just in case I got bad news. I, nonetheless, had no doubt in my mind. I knew the power my tongue carried when I prayed in faith. I trusted the God I had gotten to know and believed His every word, so I confidently gave everything away: my phone cards, my toiletries, and all of my clothes, except the ones I saved for court. I was ready to go back home.

Freedom is what we have—Christ has set us free! Stand, then, as free people, and do not allow yourselves to become slaves again.

Galatians 5:1 (GNT)

Chapter Six

THE DAY OF RECKONING

It was the morning of my court hearing. I woke up at 6 AM like I would every day. I said my morning prayer and gave thanks to God for another day, and then climbed out of my bed and began to clean my cell. I opened my cupboard, took out my clothes for court, and placed them on my bed. I then entered the tiny toilet cubicle I shared with my two cell mates – I was moved to a smaller cell since my arrival – and filled my bucket with water to have my morning wash. It wasn't Wednesday, so a proper shower wasn't an option today. But I wasn't bothered. I had already become accustomed to balancing, crouched in a bucket, and having a shallow bath with a toilet in line with my left cheek and a sink on my right; if I wasn't careful I could knock my head on either. After washing, I got dressed and redid my cornrows. By this time, my other cell mates were all also up, preparing themselves for the daily routine, which consisted of cell inspection, serving breakfast, going out to the yard, and then being locked up for the rest of the day. None of us accepted breakfast that

SEVENTY

morning. It was actually a regular thing when they would come to offer us food. We were regular fasters, so much so, rumours surfaced accusing us of being witches. We were the only black women in the prison; none of us smoked; and we were always in high spirits and singing songs in praise of God. Nobody understood our joy. That morning was a morning of immense praise and non-stop prayers. I was not in the mood for any of the enemy's antics today and left no room for him to enter. I knew he would try me, but it didn't matter because I was now strong and knew who I was in Christ. I had already refunded the mix tape of lies he had once sold me and purchased a whole catalogue of songs straight from the throne of grace.

    I didn't know what time they intended to take me to court; I just knew it was today. I also knew that I specifically asked for God to physically reign down in victory, and that by midday, I must step outside these walls and be free. They had taken my watch away from me when I arrived at the prison, so time was not something I could monitor.

    'Spazieren', the Deutsch word for 'walk', was being yelled in the hallways. It was time to go out for fresh air, socialise, and stretch our legs for a while. I decided to take the opportunity to walk the yard one last time, even though I was advised to stay in my cell until I was called to court. So there I was pacing the yard, praying, singing, and solely focusing on the finish line so close ahead.

    Suddenly, I was interrupted by a very angry voice yelling my name. Everyone paused in their tracks as I walked over to the officer, who was red in the face from shouting. She continued to shout in Deutsch in my face and I told her I didn't understand. I think that annoyed her even more, so she grabbed me by my arm and proceeded to pull me through the corridors. *So this is it then*, I thought to myself; this is where the enemy is going to try to annoy me. But as I said before, I was not in the mood to entertain the enemy's antics today – I was set on victory – so I smiled the whole way through and continued to sing to myself, ignoring the tingling feeling coming from my arm as she squeezed the blood supply to a stop. She flung me into the tiniest cell I had ever seen and slammed the door behind me. I sat there for a moment and looked at the walls around me, covered in cigarette burns, scratch marks, names, years, profanities, and drawings of devils. I had stopped singing by this moment and was reading what was written on the walls. A lot of doubtful people had clearly entered this cell before me. My heart rate began to speed up, and I thought, *what if I don't go home today?* That was enough to get me off my seat and enter prayer. It states in the book of **Ephesians 4:27**:

Don't give the Devil a chance.
(GNB)

Now certainly was not the time to let him get the upper hand because my court time had arrived. The day of reckoning was here.

I would have to say that out of all the prayers I had done during my time in prison, this prayer was and is, to this day, one I can never forget. It was a fight because every word I cried out to God was being attacked by negative thoughts, and more heavily than before. It was almost like the enemy was standing in the room with me, shouting right back at me. I moved two steps in each direction – this was how small the room was – praying until I was sweating. I declared God to be my judge and the judge in the courtroom inconsequential. I prayed that the prosecutor should not be able to speak a single negative word against me, and if they tried, they should stumble on their words. I declared God to be my councillor, and my indeed stop showering when God wants it to. I had gotten very used to seeing God in everything and witnessing Him move, so it wasn't abnormal to see and say the things I did, despite the 'she's crazy' look I was getting from my sister, which I could relate to because I was once someone with no or very little faith, and many times, smirked at those who did believe.

God was not finished proving himself faithful to me and my prayer, and just like my prayers so far – it reigning physical rain, to being outside the prison walls by 12 PM, He also honoured a prayer that I said and thought I made a mistake in saying.

I would pray daily about going home on 27 May, and one day I stumbled in prayer and said 28 May. What I panicked and thought was an accident that added more days to my time in prison was no accident at all. God is a God of no mistakes, and the spirit knows what to pray for and say even when as mere humans, we don't. I found out upon my release that my aunt and sister who flew to Austria to attend my court case were to leave to go back to the UK before me, because there were, unfortunately, no more flights available until the 28th.

SEVENTY

God had been so, so good to me; so good I even dared to pinch myself at times, as if I was dreaming. I awoke on the morning of the 28th at 6 AM, just like I would in prison, and quickly jumped out of the ever-so-comfy hotel bed and ran to the window. I pushed open the curtains, and all I saw were trees and landscaped gardens. It was a peaceful and beautiful sight. I held my mouth and began to cry. This was not a dream. I was free. My friend awoke to the sounds of my crying and asked me what was wrong. I replied, 'There's no bars on the window. We really are free.' We both sat there sobbing for a moment and then got ourselves ready to head to the airport.

God still wasn't finished showing up and showing off. In my cell after praying one day, a girl I knew from my secondary school days popped into my head. Our older sisters were friends, but she and I never forged a friendship. The only encounter we ever had was when we competed against each other in a borough sports day event and I won the race against her. I didn't understand why I thought of her that day, but she vanished as quickly as she popped into my head.

Once we arrived at the airport and checked in, we just sat on the floor and reflected on the past couple of months and how much we had gotten to know God and changed. I looked down at myself, wearing a £2,000 Louis Vuitton coat and £370 Louis Vuitton loafers, and I was unfazed by the fact that I was sitting on a dirty floor. I no longer cared about such things as I did before. I could not have a wardrobe full of expensive ready-to-wear clothes and an empty, poor soul. So whilst luxury items are nice to have, my focus had definitely shifted. It is far more important to strive for God than for worldly riches. It states in the book of **Mark 8:36**:

> ***For what shall it profit a man, if he shall gain the whole world, and lose his own soul?***
> (KJV)

While we waited for our flight, my sister called me and shared with me some sad news. Her friend's sister had just been sentenced to ten years in prison. I asked who the friend was, and she told me her name. It was the girl who I raced against and won and who had popped into my head that day. I was speechless, and again, those tiny hairs stood up all over my body. How did I manage to escape a ten-year sentence, even a ten-month sentence?

SEVENTY

And how was every single prayer request granted to me while another person received ten years – and she has children – without any mercy? Is this what it will be like on the day of judgement? Will those that believe in and have accepted Jesus Christ as their Lord and saviour and have truly repented and humbled themselves be saved; and will those that don't be stressed and tormented in hell? I didn't know enough about this girl to know whether or not she was a believer, and I trust God knew what He was doing regarding her situation, but it did make me think of the contrasting sides. However, with God's perfect track record, I did not think His word would now turn out to be a lie.

Jesus tells us in the book of **John 14:6**:

Jesus said to him, "I am the way, the truth, and the life. No one comes to the Father except through Me."
(NKJV)

So also will be the **Word** that I speak — it will not fail to do what I plan for it; it will do everything I send it to do.

Isaiah 55:11 (GNB)

Chapter Seven

GOD'S GRACIOUS GIFT

I landed back in the UK on Saturday, 28 May 2011, to smiles and hugs from my family. The questions didn't immediately flood in from them with regard to my involvement in the fraud. They were just happy to have me back. I met my boyfriend and explained what happened with his money. He was far from pleased with my explanation, and it left us in a volatile place. I wasn't sure what the outcome for us would be, but I trusted God was in control of every area of my life, so I didn't want to get back into the habit of worrying about my life or relationship. I was excited to look and move forward in the direction God wanted me to go. I knew His plan, whatever that may be, would be a good one, and He reminded me that He was indeed with me by honouring His word yet again and answering my prayer.

On Sunday, 29 May, I attended my mother's church Christian Life City, now known as iCan Ministries pastored by Bishop Wayne Malcolm. I sat there extremely nervous and almost changed my mind about delivering my testimony, but I had to remind that enemy to take a seat. This moment right then was ordained by the King himself. After hearing my name introduced, I took to the altar and stood there with the mic in my hand, delivering my testimony to a packed church – just like I told the pastor back in Austria I would be doing. When I finished, there was barely a dry eye in the house. Everyone was so excited; loud shouts of praise sounded throughout the building. One man approached me in tears. He said he had been praying to God for over 17 years and had never heard from Him until now. I didn't even know what to say. I knew God was very, very real and knew what He had done for me and through me, but I still stood there in a state of amazement that He could use little me in such a way.

I have since delivered my testimony to three other churches. Sometimes I don't even feel like I qualify, but He makes me qualified. There are times when I think I am so ready and find myself so ill-prepared, and then times when I don't think I am capable of tasks set out in front of me, and God pushes me forward and beyond where I thought I could reach.

I thought I would be a well-established fashion designer by now; married, travelling the world, and living in the house of my dreams with the white picket fence. That was at least the plan I had many years ago. The enemy has tried me in various ways, but he will never succeed. He may throw me off course and slow me down. But God still reigns supreme and will never leave or forsake me.

What God blessed me with next filled me with great joy. I was pregnant, which was an immense blessing. My boyfriend and I were not in the best place as we had both just come out of prison. Nevertheless, we were expecting a baby. I heard that people were questioning why I was having his baby, because my boyfriend was doing his own thing.

When I was around five months' pregnant, I found out that he was indeed cheating again with the same girl from before. That old feeling of insecurity started to rear its ugly head, followed by some much darker feelings. I sat on the corner of my bed. I could feel my phone constantly vibrating. I was ignoring every single phone call coming through. Only once did I answer a call from my boyfriend's friend in the hope that it would be him calling me. As soon as I knew it wasn't my boyfriend, I hung up. I was crushed. I didn't want to speak to anyone. Friends would turn up at my house banging on my door and I would ignore them.

SEVENTY

My mother turned up and I stood there, looking at her through the peephole. She told me she loved me and that she knew I was in there, and said she was coming back, but this time with the police to take the door off the hinges. I still stood there, holding my mouth, crying quietly until she left. I went back to my room and sat back on my bed. *Why am I not good enough for this man? Why is our unborn child not good enough? Why won't he love me?* In all of this, I somehow forgot that God loved me, and I started contemplating thoughts of suicide. I had some Paracetamol, which the doctors had given me to deal with the sciatica I developed as a result of the pregnancy. *I could just take them and be done*, I thought. I wouldn't have to hurt anymore, I wouldn't have to deal with the shame anymore, and he could be happy with this girl. Then I became scared of the pain I might feel from an overdose. Would it take long to die? Would I even die at all? I looked down at my stomach that was high and round and rubbed it. My rubbing turned into prodding and then squeezing. *I don't want to have his baby anymore*, I thought. *I don't want to be tied to this man who clearly does not love me.* I was then filled with immense guilt and began to cry out to God, begging for forgiveness and help. My child did not ask to be born. How dare I even think of taking my own life and rid myself of the blessing God had given me? I began to rebuke those thoughts and speak power and life into my situation. Whether or not this man loved me shouldn't be my concern. I had God who loved me, and a child due in four months. My child was no mistake even in the most unideal of situations. On 10 February 2012, I gave birth to a very healthy boy. His name is Zane.

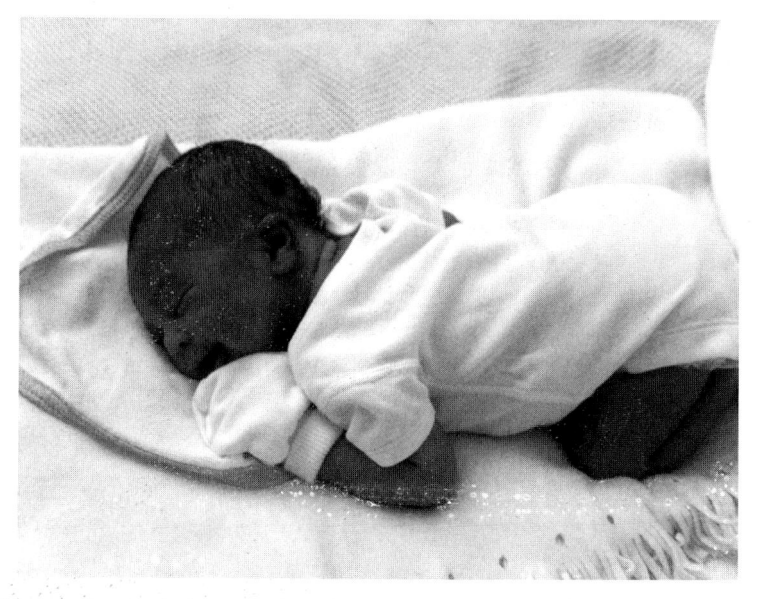

Zane /Zein/ is a name of Semitic origin [A variant of Jon from Hebrew, meaning 'God's gracious gift']

But I reckon my own life to be worth nothing to me; I only want to complete my mission and finish the work that the Lord Jesus gave me to do, which is to declare the Good News about the grace of God.

Acts 20:24 (GNB)

AFTERWORD

Four years have gone by since my experience in prison. Zane is now three, and it has taken me seven months to write this book. I wanted to write upon my release but didn't think I knew how to; plus, I was pregnant and busy trying to build my first collection for my fashion brand, so I put it off.

Putting off what God has called you to do isn't a wise decision. I didn't see myself as an author. Instead, I saw my talent in design, so I found myself ploughing money into a business that God knew I wasn't ready for. I should know by now that everything happens when and how God wants it to. I just need to do what God wants me to do and when He wants me to do it. I have since put plans for my brand on hold until the appointed time. It will happen. You will hear about it, and it will be right, just like God wants it to be.

I hope my story has blessed you all, and I pray that those with little or no faith now have reason to believe in God. Before I end, I want to share my reason for calling this book 70.

SEVENTY

I was arrested and incarcerated on 19 March 2011 and was released on 27 May 2011, a period of two months and nine days, which was approximately seventy days. God works in mysterious ways but with such precision. There are prophetic numbers within the Bible, seven representing perfection. It was in seven days that God created the Earth. God gave the Ten Commandments to let us know the order in which we should do things, thus representing perfection of divine order:

(7 perfection) X (10 perfect divine order)
=
70 perfect spiritual order

It can also represent a period of judgement. You need not take my word for it, but it says in the book of **Jeremiah 29:10-14**:

The Lord says, "When Babylonia's seventy years are over, I will show my concern for you and keep my promise to bring you back home. I alone know the plans I have for you, plans to bring you prosperity and not disaster, plans to bring about

the future you hope for. Then you will call to me. You will come and pray to me, and I will answer you. You will seek me, and you will find me because you will seek me with all your heart. Yes, I say, you will find me, and I will restore you to your land. I will gather you from every country and from every place to which I have scattered you, and I will bring you back to the land from which I had sent you away into exile. I, the Lord, have spoken."
(GNB)

How is it that after 70 days in captivity, God indeed revealed His mercy upon me and brought me back home? How is it that every time I prayed and sought God, He was there and provided me with every single thing I needed? How is it that I finished writing this book in 7 chapters and 70 pages? It is not by my power or doing. God is unquestionably who He says He is – not a god of coincidence or a god that can lie. He is the Alpha and the Omega, the Beginning and the End, and He will do everything He says He will do without faltering. He is the Perfect One and deserves all of my praise, and I cannot thank Him enough for what He has done in my life.

What God has in store for me next, I sincerely look forward to. I hope my story has served as a testament to God's mercy and grace and has shown you that no matter how dire and deep into your situation you may be, He can provide a way out. I offer encouragement to all of you to reach out to Him, and pray that in doing so, He hears and answers your prayers. God can give you the love and peace you long for, and He can heal you and restore every area of your life – if you would just trust and believe in Him. I close with this simple prayer from the book of **2 Corinthians 13:14**

The grace of the Lord Jesus Christ,
and the love of God,
and the communion of the Holy Spirit
be with you all.
(NKJV)

Now and forever more. Amen.

Saturday, 19th March, 2011

Dear Mommy,

Don't really know where to start, firstly i want to apologise for any stress your feeling for me being in prison. Secondly i want to thank you for praying for me and introducing me to God, cos that is what is helping me sleep at night and getting me through the day.
I am in Vienna, which is in Austria. I saw a judge today that says i have to wait 2 weeks for a hearing. I am being held on suspicion of fraud. I only have my bank cards on me, but they do not believe they are mine. So if in two weeks after they check the cards they turn out to be mine, my lawyer can tell them to release me. I am calm because they are my personal cards. I've not cried at all since being here and i refuse to cry and stress myself out. The prison is very very horrible and everyone speaks German or Bulgarian or some foreign language. I am in a cell with 9 other women for 23 hours, they let you out for not even a hour at 7:30am when its freezing cold to let you walk around a yard with 100's of cockroaches running around. I've had to force myself to eat small amounts of food because it's barely edible. but i cannot allow myself to succumb to this situation. They give us tea and a yoghurt for breakfast at 7am and dinner at 11am and thats it for the day!! So i gotta save the dry bread they give us and yoghurts and apple for when um starving at night. The bread is the true meaning of hard dough bread trust me lol.

When you go to church, not that you would, but do not hide my situation. I want as much prayer as possible.

When I went outside at 7am I was talking with a lady who said I must be very careful in my room because not everyone is clean! She said they can have hepatitis etc.

Cha! I've never wanted to be home so much in my life, but I try not to think about any of you to be honest, just keep praying to God and zoning out, so I don't get upset. I always knew my character was fairly strong, but this is testing it to the max, and I will not break. I've been strip searched three times and had a arrogant police officer yelling in my face for no reason. They laugh at me and I just breathe deep and talk to my father. They don't understand that our my God is a awesome God and he would never leave me or allow anything bad to happen to me. So that is very comforting and thank you again for showing me that God is the way forward, coz if I didn't know who he was, I wouldn't be coping right now.

I get canteen on a Thursday !....

To mum

Saturday 9th April 2011   Dara Knox-Hooke 331HR61/11T

Dear Dara,

I am so happy and relieve to finally here from you. I love you so much and i miss you like crazy babe stay strong and focused on getting home. I just got this letter yesterday 8, march it took a long time getting to us. but at last it here.
Dont worry about anything we are taking care of things for you.

I know where you are at the moment is not a good place but keep the faith and never give up for the Lord god is with you and he watches over you and whatever you are going through it for a greater good and he know you can handle it because we are survivors we serve an awesome and mighty god who cane do all things and make a way when it seem like there is no way so dont worry you are covered we are all praying for you, I will speak to bishop tomorrow and see if he will write to you. No weapons formed against you shall prosper so you just keep on praying and asking the lord for mercy, favour peace of mind, for his peace that surpasses all understanding you are a child of god and nothing happen to you unless he allow it this is a turning point in your life where you have to repent and change the direction that you are heading in god loves you and he is going to use you for his glory and this is your testimongg Oh my spelling is so bad it the Jamaician in me, probaly spelt Jamaician wan LoL ☺

From mum

Morning Prayer

Thank you father for waking me up this morning and watching me as I slept. I thank you for the blessings you have given me and the blessings we yet to receive.

I thank you for my current situation, as it has brought me to seek you Lord, and I pray that I can now live according to your will. I ask that you come into my heart and wash me of my sins.

Lord I thank you for my family and ask that you watch over them and comfort them. Let them come together and accept you as their Lord & Saviour.

I pray that everyone in this room will turn to you Lord, not only in times of trouble but to always have you in their thoughts and accept you as their Lord and Saviour.

I pray that we will respect one another, love one another and encourage one another to turn away from Sin.

I also pray that everyone here will learn from this and never return to jail.

Lord I pray that my boy Court Dreaming will come in spirit and ask that you their as a witness, speak through him hard in my defence so that I am pardoned at this occasion. Lord I pray that you come to cars with me, cover me and protect me, go into the hearts of the judge and prosecutor and let them have compassion towards me let them not be harsh towards me soften their hearts Lord.

Perform a miracle! So everyone will know that you alone are God and through you all things are possible.

I trust in you Lord and fear your holy name.

In the name of Jesus Christ, let me go home before Soul is done, so I can be with my family and speak of my experience in order to deter others from my mistakes.

Amen.

⑥ Went church yesterday with mum prayed as much as I could be I couldn't really concentrate because mikes kept crying and mali kept running outside but mum has been praying down the place. She was the last one at the Alter when people holding her up. The service was about Faith funnily enough. But one thing I did get from the service is that when they was saying "God has you where you are right now because he needs you in one place to work on you." And I just thought you know thats how im gonna have to see it because he has you there to work on you. He's taking you back!!! Gods like "Dave We'ii enough now"; time to come back".

Honestly Dave and im not just saying this because you are where you are *nucah screams in the background*
You are such an asset to my life never realised it this much before. And I always new I was protective over you BUT mayn you wouldn't believe me if I told you ask anyone Auntie V, num,or Anah ☺ I Love you mayn I've just been trying to handle everything like you would Left in denny you Justice. 👮 ← YOU LIKE MY DODO'S INT?

Well me sista, gotta go deal with these kids so ima leave you.

AND I'M FASTING 3 MORE HOURS TO GO!!!

Love you more then you can imagine

Lov Lov
♡♡♡

Prisoner hnr 111213

God, no matter what you are going through God is bigger than this he would shall see you through it, what you are going through right now is just a testimony there is no testimony without a "TEST" and there is no trial without a "TRIBULATION" sometimes when depart from God he allows us to go into a mess so he can send us "MESSAGE" that this is the only time where you can now only totally depend on me but no one else, because it states in the bible that God is a jealous God and when you don't put him first he would allow certain things to happen so he can show you that the only way for you to come out of it is to not totally depend on him, trust in God Dara he would make a way when it seems like there is no way, this is not your purpose to be lock up like your some animal you are a very smart and beautiful girl you have so much for yourself. Just continue to trust in God totally trust in him you are his daughter he said "he would never leave us or forsake us" he said weapon shall form but shall not prosper, remember his word when you are praying remind him of what he said to us that his word cannot return unto us valid. I know you most probably can't phone me but I'm going to send a prayer for you through this letter

Father in the name of your son Jesus Christ I come to you giving you all the glory, honour and praise because you alone are worthy of the praise, father God I thank you for everything you have done in my life and Dara life, Father God I thank you for allowing me and Dara to continue to have our friendship father God you know that every night when I pray I ask you to remove people from my life that will hinder me from serving you so I thank you God that she is still in my life and she can see my light shine so I can be an example for her, Father God you know that the enemy has made plans against your daughter but Father God I ask you to have mercy upon her life right now, whatever the enemy has made for evil Father God I ask you to turn it around for good let this test be a testimony let this mess be a message to her, Father God you said that weapon shall form but they shall not prosper so every weapon that the enemy has plan over her life I come against it in the precious blood of Jesus, she is a woman of God she shall serve you Father God and be the woman of God that you ordained her to be every plan that the enemy has set against we come against it with the precious of blood of Jesus, Father God at this moment of time watch over her send your holy spirit to comfort her send your angels to guide the four corners of her sell, protect her from all evil and the plan of the enemy. Show yourself to her Father God and let her know that you are the true and living God and that no one shall have the true joy, love and peace if they don't have you as their Lord and Saviour for your word says "what does it profit a man if he gains the whole world and loses his soul". Father God we trust you we love you and adore you, we are totally depending on you, not man but you Father God because you hold the world in your hand, Father God we leave everything totally in your hands and we thank you for what you have done so far in our lives and we thank you in advance because we know that you are a God that never fails us, so we thank you for the total victory, in Jesus name we pray.

AMEN......

Love you girl